Contents

Introduction   3

How to Use This Workbook   7

Day 1: The power in your thoughts   9

Day 2: Flip those thoughts   15

Day 3: Making loving and kind thoughts a daily habit   19

Day 4: Breakthrough your limitations   25

Day 5: Take action with your new thoughts   30

Day 6: Affirmations repeated!   36

Day 7: Imagining your wildest dreams   42

Day 8: See it to believe it!   46

Day 9: Fuel for success   54

Day 10: What is our Spirit?   61

Day 11: What is intuition?   68

Day 12: Building a relationship with your intuition   73

Day 13: Attitude of gratitude   77

Day 14: Stop "shoulding" all over yourself!!   82

Day 15: Stillness Speaks   89

Day 16: Meditation for daily living   94

Day 17: Money worries – how to change the script!   101

Day 18: Decisions, decisions, decisions!   109

Day 19: Everyday kindness   120

Day 20: Daily mindfulness   129

Day 21: Ask for help   136

Final thoughts and wishes   142

Introduction

Welcome to the *SOUL SIDE UP* Workbook- *HOW to make "self-help" work for YOU in your daily life.*

This workbook is designed to complement the *SOUL SIDE UP* Workshops that are being held in venues worldwide but it can also be used without having to attend the course, in the comfort of your own home.

The purpose of this workbook is to give *you,* the participant, the tools and lessons to help create happiness, joy, purpose and meaning in your daily life. The workbook is designed to give you simple yet effective exercises that work on the body, mind and soul.

The workbook is designed to be done over 21 days and each day has different daily exercises to create positive and lasting change in your life.

The exercises and teachings in this book *will* create positive and lasting changes in your life if you choose to allow the change and growth. No book can change you. You are far more powerful than any book. *YOU* can change you. We just need to learn HOW to make the changes and be reminded of the power that is within.

Think of the word **HOW** as you work through this book. Whenever you think; "How do I make the changes?" or

"How do I do this?", take the word **HOW** and break it down.

H

Honest with yourself as you face your true self in all its glory and brilliance.

O

Openness. Be open to let go of old thoughts, beliefs, behaviours and habits that are no longer serving you. Be open to receive and let in, new thoughts, beliefs, love and abundance, that will want to come to you when you make the changes.

W

Willingness. Be willing to do the work. Be willing to give yourself time to learn and make changes. Be willing to believe that anything you want to change within you, you can. Be willing to believe that you deserve to feel happy, you deserve to have a life you dream of, you deserve to feel joy every day. You are worthy of a life you love, today, exactly as you are.

These daily exercises have been tried and tested by the thousands of clients I have worked with in my practice as an intuitive life coach and I have tested them in all areas of my own life and continue to do so on a daily basis. I have seen incredible results when the client uses these exercises to make simple changes and shifts in their daily lives.

In order for us to feel happiness, joy and meaning in our lives, we need to become aware of that, which is in our control; our thoughts, behaviours and actions so that they are in alignment with the vibration and energy of happiness, joy and abundance. These changes may be very small and seem so simple but it is amazing what a small change in perspective or in how we act can bring incredible and life changing results.

We are very lucky to live in a time where we have access to so much information on how to be happier and healthier. There are thousands of books that show us and teach us how to 'SELF-HELP". I believe, that in order to see and feel happiness, love and abundance we have to make it a conscious daily choice and practice. We have to put into action what we learn and make it a part of our everyday lives. This will involve changing behaviours and thoughts that we may have had for years and years, this isn't easy, but we all have the ability and power to do it and the rewards are immeasurable. If we just *think* about changing, read all the books, but never take action, having a life that we love will just be a great idea that we never actually get to experience. Happiness, love and joy are meant to be experienced and felt, not stay as some concept in our minds. If we don't know how to take the information that we learn and bring it into our daily lives, we will never see the great ideas work and never get to feel and experience love and abundance, this to me, is a waste.

I hope that this workbook brings the concept of happiness, love, peace and joy and makes it a reality that you can feel and experience as you move through your day, whatever your day looks like. My wish for you all, is that you realise that the power to create your life so that it is filled with love and happiness, is right there within you. The power just needs to be used and practiced everyday, small changes daily will create the life you dream of. May you feel the positive loving energy that created this book and may that same energy fill your life and bring you the happiness and joy that you deserve. I hope that this book brings you on a wonderful journey of self-discovery, a journey that you can re-visit time and time again and pass on to others. Watch and see what happens, believe and trust and just take it one day at a time....one moment at a time...every moment is a chance to begin again!

I will be sharing my own personal journey and story as to how I have used the following exercises, created miracles in my life and ultimately gone from a place of fear to love in my upcoming book soon to be released on my life story. You can find all the information on my website **www.georginadurcan.com**

How to Use This Workbook

What you will need:

- An open heart and mind.

- A special journal to write in.

- A few different colour pens.

- Willingness.

- A smile.

- 5-10 minutes of time for you every day.

  Most importantly for this process remember the word **H.O.W. HOW** embodies all the qualities we need for real change in our lives.

- **H** - Honesty

- **O** - Openness

- **W** - Willingness.

  Just ask yourself am I prepared to be honest, open and willing?

The SOUL SIDE UP workbook is your daily companion to bring you happiness and love.

You can choose to follow the workbook from Day 1 to Day 21, select a day at random or pick a day that may cover an area you wish to work on. There is no right and wrong way, whatever feels right for you on the day!

The exercise that you do every day brings love, happiness, joy and abundance into your life as an action.

I would encourage you to complete every exercise in the book as there is purpose and meaning behind every exercise and they have all been infused and created with so much love! You can repeat the exercises as often as you feel is right for you and let this book be there for you when you need it. My hope is that this book becomes a daily companion that you carry with you, to help and support you with the daily challenges life can bring. We can't stop the daily challenges but we can learn how to move through them with greater confidence, ease and happiness.

If you feel like you need extra support on this journey I encourage you to attend one of the live SOUL SIDE UP workshops, where you will have group support and encouragement and also a whole lot of fun!

Day 1: The power in your thoughts

"If you correct the mind the rest of your life will fall into place" - Lao Tzu

You have a power within that has the ability to complete transform your experience of life. Everyone has it and it is with you always. It can be your greatest friend or your most destructive enemy. For most of us, we don't fully know how to tap into this power and use it to create a life that we dream of. This power is contained within your thoughts and beliefs.

Your mind is made up of thoughts and beliefs. We have approximately 60,000 thoughts a day, 98% are repeats from the day before and 85% are subconscious. It is hard to believe that we have 60,000 thoughts a day, no wonder we don't get a moments peace! These thoughts make up our internal chatter, the monkey mind, some of it we are aware of, and some, is subconscious. We need to build our self-awareness in order to be able to fully utilise the power in our thoughts to create a life we love. When we become aware, of the dominating thoughts and beliefs, that are creating our daily experience of life, we then have an opportunity to change what is not working for us. We will be aware of the thoughts that are not serving us and replace them with ones that will generate the power, to create a life we love.

Thoughts create energy, that energy then, creates feelings in the body and that, in turn, becomes what we experience. Our thoughts send out a lot of energy into the universe, so they not only affect us, they affect others too. Different thoughts have different vibrations. These vibrations can actually be measured in the body, for example, guilt has a very low vibration and will bring our energy to a low place, this then puts an energy out into the world and others can feel it too. If others can feel our energy, that will affect our interactions and experiences on a daily basis. Calm thoughts or optimistic thoughts, on the other hand, have a very high vibration, which is uplifting for ourselves and others. This vibration will create very uplifting and positive experiences on a daily basis. Believe it or not, we have the ability to choose what thoughts we want to think. Right now, you may not be aware of the thoughts you think and what vibration they are producing, hopefully by the end of this workbook you will be able to use the powerful energy in your thoughts to create the experience of life that you desire.

In order to start choosing thoughts and beliefs that support, nourish and uplift you in life, we need to understand and become more aware of what thoughts and beliefs are and then become aware of the thoughts and beliefs that are limiting us. Over the next few days, if you complete the exercises, you will learn exactly what your dominant thoughts are, whether they are limiting you or not and which ones you will choose to change.

A belief is a thought we have repeated. The mind learns there must be value in the particular thought as you have repeated it daily, many times in a day and possibly over the course of many years. It started as a thought that you learnt or interpreted, you repeated it enough times for the mind to take notice, it interprets this as something you want to hold onto, and so that is exactly what it does by forming a belief. A belief is a thought that the mind takes seriously and takes it as a fact, which actually began as a simple thought or interpretation you had about something.

All our beliefs make up our belief system. Our belief system is what we act from every day, it influences our behaviour, our decisions and our choices and therefore creates the life we are experiencing. If we act from our belief system every day and it is creating the reality we are experiencing we want to become very aware of what our belief system is. If our belief system is creating a life that is not moving us towards our goals and dreams we need to change it. To change a belief system we must become very aware of what it is.

"The happiness in your life depends on the quality of your thoughts"

Over the course of this workbook we are going to become very aware, of how we are using the amazingly powerful gifts and tools within us. If we are using them to create a life we desire then we are going to feel fulfilled, on purpose in life and happy. If on the other hand we are using our gifts within to push ourselves further away from the life we want, then we want to identify what is not working and believe we have the power to change it. Throughout this workbook, by doing the exercises, you are learning how to change whatever is not supporting you in your life.

When something is not the way we would like it to be in our lives, we try and change the outside, the external. We often try and change other people's behaviours, their actions towards us, our boss's behaviours, the banks and so on. The most frustrating part in trying to change the external, is that, we have no control over other people's thoughts and behaviours, as much as we might try, if they don't want to change, we can't make them change. We don't have control over other people's thoughts, behaviours and actions, yet we expend so much energy trying to control these things. When we actually start focusing our energy on that which is within our control, has such an effect on our daily life, and creates our daily experience, we will be able to create a life that we can enjoy and love. Focusing and taking responsibility of our thoughts, beliefs and actions will produce the results that we desire. Is that not a better use of our energy and time?

The 3 things we have control of in life

- The thoughts we think
- The images we visualise
- The actions we take

How you use those 3 things determines your experience of life. Let us see how we can use those 3 things, to create the feelings and experiences in life that we truly desire.

"The primary cause of unhappiness is never the situation but your thoughts about it" - Eckhart Tolle

Exercise 1

Awareness of my thoughts

1. Write 10 thoughts you have about yourself regularly.

Example: *"I am overweight" "I am not a good enough partner" "I get angry too easily"*

When you have written the thoughts about yourself ask yourself these questions:

Are these thoughts lifting me up?

Are these thoughts encouraging and motivating me?

Are these thoughts making me feel afraid?

Are these kind thoughts?

Would I speak this way to someone I love?

Are these thoughts compassionate and understanding?

When you have reflected on these questions, pick out the thoughts that pull you down, that demotivate you, that criticise and judge and leave you feeling afraid.

We can change these thoughts to ones that empower and uplift you. When we change the thing that has the greatest influence over how our day feels and looks, we are tapping into a power within us that can totally change your experience of life.

"The thought manifests as the word. The word manifests as the deed. The deed develops into habit. And the habit hardens into character. So watch the thought and its ways with care. And let it spring from love, born out of concern for all beings." – Buddha

In exercise 2 you will see how to change the thoughts.

Day 2: Flip those thoughts

As we learnt in day 1, we have 60,000 thoughts a day on average and roughly 98% are repeats from the day before. Repeated thoughts have incredible power on our physical, mental and emotional experiences. When we repeat something we place value on it and we are investing a lot of mental, physical and emotional energy into it. This energy goes out into the universe and an experience and feeling comes back to match that energy.

As we have also seen, we can learn how to control our thoughts by becoming more aware of what your repeated thoughts are and then assessing whether they are helping you in life or not.

When we have awareness of our repeated thoughts, we can decide whether they are moving us closer or further away from our desired feelings and life experiences.

We have the ability to choose the thoughts we think, when we choose thoughts that are kinder, more compassionate, more understanding and more loving towards ourselves, we actually *FEEL* kinder, more loving, more understanding and compassionate towards ourselves and others.

Imagine how it would feel, to have the most loving kind voice you can imagine, supporting and encouraging you, 24 hours a day, every day!!

You can have this. It is within us all. We just need to turn the volume up on that voice within, to be able to hear it, feel it and experience it. You can start today!

Let us begin

Exercise 2

Turn fear to love

Repeat this phrase/affirmation before you begin this exercise:

"I choose to reinterpret my negative and fearful thoughts with a more loving perspective"

Take your thoughts from exercise 1 that are negative, fearful or pull your energy down.

We are now going to change them into thoughts that are positive, uplifting, kind and loving

Read one of your negative thoughts from exercise 1. Say it out loud. Hear how it sounds and notice how it feels in your body as you say it.

Now think of someone you love deeply. If they told you, what their fearful thought was, think of what you would say to them, to encourage, uplift and help them feel loved.

Write down what you would say to your loved one about each of your thoughts.

These are your new thoughts, which you are now going to turn around and direct at yourself.

Example:

My negative fearful thought: **"I am never going to pay off my debts"**

What I would say to a loved one: **"It will all be cleared in time because you deserve to enjoy life and deserve to have abundance and the money you need to enjoy life"**

New positive loving kind thought for me: **"I am deserving of financial freedom and to have the money to do the things I love"**

If you can put the words I AM at the beginning of your new thought, it gives it a lot more energy, as you are confirming this as the truth of who you are. We will discuss the power of the words I AM in later exercises.

Do the above process with all the negative thoughts from exercise 1. You will then have a list, of new, loving, kind, supportive and encouraging thoughts that are moving you closer and closer to the feelings you want to feel and the life you desire.

In exercise 3 we will look at how to make these new loving thoughts part of your daily routine.

Day 3: Making loving and kind thoughts a daily habit

As we have seen, thoughts that are repeated daily create very powerful energy, which will in turn effect how we feel, how we behave and what experiences we attract into our lives. We have also seen that the thoughts we repeat, become our beliefs, which make up our belief system, which the mind then interprets as fact, and then creates experiences to match. We will look at our beliefs in more detail on day 4 and 5.

We have also learnt, that we can become aware of our thoughts, and choose to change them if they are not serving us. We can create new loving, kind and supportive thoughts to replace the ones that are creating a life experience that we don't wish for. This is what we did in exercise 2, and the more we practice flipping the negative thought to a positive, we are training our mind, through repetition, that we consciously choose the positive thoughts, that these are the ones we value. The mind then sets about creating daily life experiences to match the thoughts that you have repeated.

In order for the new thoughts, that we wrote out in exercise 2, to have great energy and power in our lives, we must repeat them often enough, for the mind to take them in as truth and then start to create experiences to match. We need to affirm to the Universe every day that this is what we value and this is how we want to feel.

"Our subconscious minds have no sense of humour, play no jokes and cannot tell the difference between reality and an imagined thought or image. What we continually think about eventually will manifest in our lives." – Robert Collier

We affirm and repeat the new thoughts using **affirmations.**

Affirmations affirm the goal or dream as if it is already here in reality. This programmes the mind to create these thoughts to become your new daily experience.

Affirmations are thoughts that are in alignment with your goals and dreams. If repeated they will tell your subconscious mind what to create in your life.

Exercise 3

How to create powerful affirmations:

1. Start with the words I AM. The subconscious mind takes these words very seriously. It is affirming the highest possible truth. The mind interprets this as a fact.

    - Use the present tense

    - Affirm what you want, not what you don't want

    - Keep it brief and specific

    - Include at least one emotion/feeling

2. Take the loving kind thoughts that you created in exercise 2.

3. Following the guidelines above we are going to make them into powerful affirmations.

Example:

My new loving thought is: **"I deserve to have a body that I love and feel good with"**

Affirmation: **"I AM loving and feeling great in my body today"**

4. Try and do this with all your loving thoughts. Don't worry too much about getting the wording right, the universe knows what you mean!

5. You now have a list of positive, loving, motivating and supportive affirmations to create a life you love. Put this list in your phone, your daily diary, on your bathroom mirror or fridge, place it somewhere you can see it daily and many times during the day.

6. First thing in the morning as you open your eyes, read your list and repeat out loud if possible or silently in your mind.

7. Last thing at night before you go to sleep recite your list again.

8. As many times as you can during your day, recite and read your list. Some people put an alarm on their smartphone at certain times to remind them to read and recite their affirmations.

9. If you become aware that your mind is in a fearful, negative or worrisome state, recite your list of positive loving affirmations, this will not only shift the negative energy, it will also train your mind that when fear and negativity comes in, we choose the love instead!

Examples of positive affirmations:

I AM willing to see love.

I AM willing to let go of all my self-doubt

I AM love

I AM grateful for my amazing body

I AM totally open to receive a wonderful new job that I love

I AM working with people that love and respect me.

I AM always doing the very best that I can in everything that I do

I AM enjoying a loving and supportive relationship with my partner

I AM healthy, whole and complete

I AM open to receive all the abundance the world has to give me

"Your subconscious mind does not argue with you. It accepts what your conscious mind decrees. If you say "I can't afford it" your subconscious mind works to make it true" - Dr Joseph Murray

Day 4: Breakthrough your limitations

"The only limits you have are the limits you believe" - Dr Wayne Dyer

Our belief system is what we act from every day, it influences our behaviour, our decisions and our choices and therefore creates the life we are experiencing. Beliefs are thoughts we have repeated, through repetition, the mind learns to value them and then locks them in as beliefs. Most of our beliefs are created from age of 2-8.

If we act from our belief system every day, and it is creating the reality we are experiencing, we want to become very aware of what our belief system is. If our belief system is creating a life that is not moving us towards our goals and dreams, we need to change it. To change a belief system we must become very aware of what it is, just like we became very aware of our thoughts in the previous exercises.

We need to become aware of our beliefs, that are limiting how we experience life now, and what is possible for us to experience in the future.

Beliefs create very powerful energy. The mind sees great value in the beliefs because we have repeated them so often, so a lot of energy is produced when we think of them. This energy in turn, creates feelings in the body which creates a vibration, we then attract similar energy back to us. Most of our beliefs are subconscious, we need to make them conscious and become aware of them, as they have a powerful effect on our lives. We want to be able to harness that power and make our beliefs work for us to create the life we desire. We can tell the subconscious what we want to believe, therefore creating energy that will attract happiness, love and abundance.

Limiting beliefs are beliefs that are limiting your potential and blocking your ability to live the life you dream of. Limiting beliefs stop us even taking the first steps towards creating a life we dream of. Limiting beliefs stop us taking action, they stop us in believing that change is possible and that we can achieve our goals and dreams. Moving beyond your limiting beliefs is critical for success. The wonderful and incredible thing about our mind, is that, it will do what we consciously tell it to do. We have the power and ability to remove our limiting beliefs. We do this, by first becoming aware of what our limiting beliefs are and then replacing them with the beliefs that are going to support us in achieving a life we love. In today's exercise we will become aware of our limiting beliefs, awareness is the first step in trying to change anything.

"When you change what you believe, you change what you do… which changes what you get." – Odille Rault

Exercise 4

The limits are all in my head!

1. Let's become aware of some of your limiting beliefs. Think about a dream or goal you have. Now think about trying to achieve it. What does your mind say to you when you think about it being possible? For example: Dream is: "I would love to get married", Belief that comes up when I think of my dream: "There is no one out there that will love me the way I want to be loved" In part 2, answer the questions below, if you struggle to hear what your limiting belief is, think of your goal as we did here and listen to the limiting voice that comes after it.

2. •   My limiting belief is ....

    •   The way it limits me is ....

    •   The way I want to be, act or feel is ....

    •   My new belief or turnaround statement is.....................

Example:

My limiting belief is ... "I am not good enough to attract someone who will love me"

The way it limits me is ... I don't talk to anyone that I am attracted to because I believe they won't like me.

The way I want to be, act or feel is ... I want to feel confident and attractive and to be able to approach people that I am attracted to without feeling like I am going to be rejected.

My new belief or turnaround statement is ... I am an attractive, confident, beautiful person with so much love to give. I know that I deserve to feel this way in all that I do and the person that I am approaching will see the beautiful person I am.

3. When you catch yourself thinking the old limiting belief, stop, take a breath and repeat the new belief (out loud if possible)

4. This new thought repeated, will become a belief, and you will now be able to take steps forward because the new believe allows your mind to realise that your dreams are possible. This new belief will affect how you feel, your energy, vibration and what you attract back into your life through the external experiences. Your beliefs hugely impact your day to day feelings and experiences.

5. If you find you are resisting saying the new belief, repeat this

    "Today I welcome new perceptions. I am willing to let go of my old limiting beliefs and let the loving belief enter in. I choose to believe that there is always a loving kind perspective"

6. Remember the choice of what you believe is up to you.

Day 5: Take action with your new thoughts

We have looked at how our thoughts and beliefs may be stopping us from creating a life we love. We have learnt how to change the thoughts and beliefs that are not supporting our dreams and goals. Before we move towards achieving a goal, we need to make sure we have thoughts and beliefs to support the goal. If a goal of mine is to run a marathon but I have a limiting belief of: "I am not good enough so there is no point in entering" or "I am not good at sports", do you think I am going to take action to move towards the goal? Are those beliefs and thoughts making it easy for me to step forward? Those limiting beliefs create a lot of fear of failing and fear of taking a risk, the more fear that is generated in our minds, the harder and harder it is to move forward and take a step towards achieving our goals.

When we begin to think about what our goals and dreams are in life, we are probably going to meet resistance from the beginning, as our limiting beliefs show up to stop us. Early childhood programming gets in the way of even letting us think about what we want from life. We learn very early on in life, about what is possible for us, this may be learning from our parents or what we experienced around us. We start to form beliefs about what is possible for us, and what we "should" believe in and what we "should" do with our lives.

A teacher in school may have said; "I don't think art is your best subject" and how, we may interpret that, is, "I am no good at art". This thought is repeated and then forms a limiting belief that sounds like "I am not creative or arty". This belief will stick and when opportunities come up to try something creative, we will hear this limiting belief and stop ourselves from trying in case we fail. We then never get to test out the theory whether the belief is actually correct or not.

"Nothing is impossible, the word itself says I'm Possible"
- Audrey Hepburn

We also learn early on in our lives, what pleases our parents and how we need to behave in order to be loved, we can form beliefs from this learning. We may learn that we need to get a job like the one our parents have to be happy and successful, we see that this is possible, because our parents are doing it and we may believe that that needs to be our path too. This learning forms believes about what your dreams should be. We mould our dreams around, what we think will meet our parents and our peers approval. This can lead to people never trying to create a life that they wish for, out of fear of what people will think or believing it is not possible.

In today's exercise we are going to start breaking through what our mind believes is   possible. We are going to start creating goals, and taking steps towards achieving them. The mind is now, going to have to let go of its limiting beliefs and actually see what truly is possible. The only way that we see what is possible, is taking small steps consistently. We have to take action, however small, in order to see our dreams and goals manifest. Once the mind starts to see results, it starts to believe, and when we believe, it makes it easier and easier to take more and more steps because we don't have the same fears and limitations.

"The greatest danger for most of us is not that our aim is too high and we miss it but that it is too low and we reach it" - Michaelangelo

Exercise 5

GOALS GOALS GOALS!!

1. Using your imagination, if anything was possible, write goals in each of following areas: Financial, Career, Free time, Health, Community and Relationships.

2. When writing your goals, don't let the mind tell you what you "should" write, or what would make others happy, these goals have to light you up from the inside out, they have to be YOUR dreams and goals.

3. When you are writing your goals in each of the areas above, make sure your goals are measurable (How much and by when), use dates and times and things you can measure. Vague goals produce vague results.

4. What will bring these goals to you, and how will you reach them? The answer, is to take ACTION. To achieve a goal, one thing is certain, you will have to get out of your comfort zone. To achieve a goal we

have to stretch ourselves, push through our limiting beliefs and fears, this feels uncomfortable but that is what makes it a challenge. When we overcome a challenge, the exhilaration, confidence, inner strength and belief we acquire is unimaginable and so worth getting out of your comfort zone for.

5. What stops you taking action? - Limiting beliefs, thoughts, fears and external obstacles. Fear is our greatest block to taking action towards our goals. Fears are created in the mind from our thoughts and limiting beliefs. Fear, will be there when we start pushing through our self-imposed limitations, but if we make an action plan, that maps out the steps we need to take, to achieve our goals, it makes the fear manageable. With each step that we take, the fear gets quieter and quieter until it is just a whisper and then we are well on our way!

6. Take one goal from each of the areas and map out an action plan.

    For example:

    Goal: To run 10km by December

    Action plan: Week 1 May 1st - 7th

                         Walk fast for 20 minutes everyday

                         Week 2 may 8th - 13th

Walk fast for 25 minutes everyday

Break your goal down into specific times and action steps. The mind starts to release fear when it can see the plan all mapped out! The mind doesn't like uncertainty.

7. When you have an action plan written for each goal, pin it up somewhere you can see it every day and make sure you tick off each action step when you have achieved it. Celebrate each action taken, however small the step, each step is getting you closer and closer to living a life you love.

8. You can also create affirmations to support each of your goals. We will be looking at affirmations in more detail on Day 6 and in the days following, there will be more techniques to help make your dreams a reality.

"Take the first step even though you don't see the staircase" - Martin Luther King Jr

Day 6: Affirmations repeated!

I know you are thinking; "Hey, I have already worked on affirmations, why am I doing it again?!!" Trust me, I am not running out of things to say, there is a reason for the repetition!!

I cannot emphasise enough, how important it is to get our thoughts and beliefs, supporting and working with us to create our dreams, rather than de-motivating us and putting us down with harsh judgements and criticisms. Repetition and forming positive daily habits will create transformational differences in your life. What we repeatedly think, we repeatedly feel and that in turn creates our daily habits which we then act from. So I am repeating myself with this daily exercise with an intention to bring these positive and loving thoughts into your daily life, everyday! The following exercise will start making affirmations a daily practice, which *will* produce miracles! Speaking of miracles, one of my daily affirmations is, "I AM a magnet for miracles" and believe me, you are too!

- Affirmations are an important part of manifesting and bringing your dreams from imagination to reality.

- The biggest block to achieving our goals and dreams is our limiting and fearful beliefs. They stop us taking action. We need to create beliefs and thoughts that will manifest our dreams. Our thoughts, beliefs and the words we speak have very powerful energy and if they are not aligned with our dreams, we feel stuck and defeated. Affirmations help to get our thoughts and beliefs aligned with the life we desire and dream of. Trust me, getting your mind, your most powerful tool, on your side, working towards and in the direction of your dreams, is the best gift you can ever give yourself.

- Affirmations affirm the goal or dream as if it's already here in reality. This programmes the mind towards creating the dreams to be a reality in your life.

- Affirmations, if repeated, will tell your subconscious mind what to create in your life.

Everything is vibration. Positive vibration feels uplifting, negative vibration feels deflating. So as you create, say, or write affirmations, be sure they feel uplifting to you. As you begin to embody these affirmations and believe them, you will start attracting what you desire. Affirmations will raise your vibration and the optimistic and positive language will help remove fear and doubt. The more you tell yourself something, the more you will believe it. You can choose to imprint positive, self-affirming beliefs instead of negative, self-defeating beliefs. YOU CAN CHOOSE.

"A man is but the product of his thoughts. What he thinks he becomes. – Gandhi"

Using the same guidelines from day 3, we will create affirmations to support your goals:

- Start with the words, **I AM** - the subconscious mind takes these words very seriously and the words **I AM** is a creative force unlike any other!

- Use the present tense

- Affirm what you want not what you don't want

- Keep it brief and specific

- Include at least one emotion/feeling. As you are saying your affirmations try and imagine how it would feel to achieve them. Imagine the emotions you would feel.

Exercise 6

Affirm your goals into reality

- Take the goals you wrote on day 5.

- Create affirmations that state the goals as if they have already been achieved.

   For example;

   Goal: To have 10 new clients by the end of December

   Affirmation: "I AM working with 10 new clients and I AM attracting new clients every month with ease"

- Take a limiting belief/ fear from day 4 and create an affirmation that flips the fear.

   For example;

   Limiting belief: "I am not good enough to get the promotion in work"

   Affirmation: "I AM confident and deserving to be recognised, valued and appreciated in work, promotions and bonuses come to me in divine perfect timing"

- Repeat your affirmations every day for at least 30days.

- Put the list of affirmations somewhere you will see it repeatedly throughout your day, for example; on the fridge, your screensaver, on a bathroom mirror and so on.

Examples of some affirmations.

1. I AM receiving abundance now in expected and unexpected ways.

2. I AM increasingly confident in my ability to create the life I desire.

3. I AM acting on inspiration and insights and I trust my inner guidance.

4. I AM giving and receiving all that is good and all that I desire.

5. I AM receiving infinite, inexhaustible and immediate abundance.

6. I AM creating my life according to my dominant beliefs; and I AM improving the quality of those beliefs.

7. I AM constantly striving to raise my vibration through good thoughts, words and actions.

8. I AM making a meaningful contribution to the world and I AM wonderfully compensated for my contribution.

9. I AM willing to believe that I AM the creator of my life experience.

10. I AM willing to believe that by raising my vibration, I will attract more of what I desire.

11. I AM willing to believe that by focusing on feeling good, I make better choices that lead to desired results.

12. I AM worthy of love, abundance, success, happiness and fulfilment.

Day 7: Imagining your wildest dreams

- You have created your goals on day 5, created affirmations and beliefs to support them, now we need to really imprint these goals in the subconscious mind by using images.

- A picture speaks a 1000 words.

- The mind is like a GPS, it needs the coordinates to be specific so it can move clearly to where it is told to go.

- Images activate the creative powers of your subconscious mind

- The mind, when it has a clear image and picture of your goals, sets about attracting the people, resources and opportunities that are needed to achieve your goal.

- When you visualise your goal, as if it is completed, it creates "Structural Tension". This "tension", is where the mind wants to move you, from where you are presently, towards the goal/image.

- The mind will seek out your vision and capture all the information and resources necessary to bring it into reality.

Exercise 7

- Morning and night read your goals/affirmations (out loud preferably).

- Pause after each affirmation/goal, close your eyes and create a visual image of the goal completed.

- Imagine sights, sounds, smells and emotions.

- Do this with each goal.

- 1 hr of visualisation = 7 hrs physical effort

- If you like, you can create your own goal book. Write all your goals out in a journal. Add images and pictures of your goals that you have cut out from magazines etc.

Many people are using Pinterest now to create vision boards of their dreams and goals. We will look at how to create your own vision board on day 8.

If you really want to start your day, in the best way possible to create a life you love, then try having a "POWER HOUR"!

- POWER HOUR:

    - 20 mins doing affirmations and visualising your goals as completed

    - 20 mins exercise

    - 20 mins inspirational reading

If your lifestyle doesn't allow for an hour, try to even do 5mins on each section. Believe me, even 5 minutes a day can make a profound difference in your daily life.

Day 8: See it to believe it!

Creating a vision book is probably one of the most valuable visualisation tools available to you. This powerful tool serves as your vision and picture of the future - a tangible representation of where you are going. It represents your dreams, your goals, and your ideal life. When your mind can see clearly where you are going, it helps the mind to believe it is real and not just in the imagination. As we said in the previous exercise, images activate the creative powers of your subconscious mind. The mind responds strongly to visual stimulation. In the previous exercises you have defined your dreams and goals, now we get to illustrate them visually.

How to create a Vision Book:

1. Find pictures that represent or symbolise the experiences, feelings, and possessions you want to attract into your life, and place them in your book. Use photographs, magazine cut-outs, pictures from the Internet--whatever inspires you. Cut out pictures that when you look at them you feel excited and inspired. Don't try and plan in your mind what you are going to choose, let yourself be guided to whatever speaks to you as

you are looking at the magazines etc. Before I begin, I ask my angels and my spirit to guide me to the pictures that are my true desires and then I just have fun with it!

2. You might also want to put your affirmations, inspirational words, quotations, and thoughts here. Choose words and images that inspire you and make you feel good.

3. Use the words and images that best represent your purpose, your ideal future, and words that inspire positive emotions in you. There is beauty in simplicity and clarity. Too many images and too much information will be distracting and harder to focus on.

4. Some people prefer to put all the images on a big board and pin it up where they can see it daily. It doesn't matter which you choose, it is whatever you feel more comfortable with, and that is easiest for you to look at every day.

5. Write the date on the vision book or board as you will be amazed when you look back and see how the Universe has responded to your commitment and energy.

How to use your Vision Book:

1. Try keeping your vision book next to your bed. Try and spend time each morning and evening visualising, affirming, believing, and internalising your goals.

2. The time you spend visualising in the evening just before bed is especially powerful. The thoughts and images that are present in your mind during the last forty-five minutes before going to sleep are the ones that will replay themselves repeatedly in your subconscious mind throughout the night, and the thoughts and images that you begin each day with will help you to create a vibration and energy for the day and life that you desire.

3. Look at your vision book often and feel the excitement and positive energy it provides.

4. Look at the images and really feel the future it represents.

5. Read your affirmations and inspirational words aloud.

6. Believe it is going to happen. If you struggle with this part create affirmations as we did in the previous exercises to encourage your mind to believe. Example: "I AM willing to believe that I AM the creator of my life experience"

7. Be grateful for the good that is already present in your life. We will look at gratitude and how to bring that into your life later on in the workbook.

8. Acknowledge any goals you have already achieved.

9. Acknowledge the changes you have seen and felt.

10. As your dreams begin to manifest, look at those images that represent your achievements, and feel gratitude for how well your commitment and energy is working in your life. Acknowledge that it is working. Don't remove the pictures or images that represent the goals you've already achieved. Achievement of the goals in your

vision book are powerful reminders of what you have already consciously and deliberately attracted into your life. We all have days where we doubt if our dreams are possible and if any changes are actually happening, we sometimes get impatient because we haven't seen the changes in the time that we wanted, having your vision book to hand during those times is very powerful. As you look through the book, your negative energy will begin to shift and you will be reminded of the dreams that have been achieved, it will reinstate your belief in yourself and that your dreams are possible, we forget to acknowledge how much we have actually grown, changed and what we achieve and conquer on a daily basis. Visual reminders of how amazing we actually are, make a huge difference in our daily life.

11. This book will document your personal journey, your dreams, and your achievements. You will want to keep it and reflect back upon it in years to come. I recommend creating a new vision book each year because as we grow and change, your

dreams will too. Years later, as you look back on your vision books, you will be amazed about how much has actually come into creation, sometimes we don't notice at the time and its only years later that we realise how accurately we manifested our dreams.

Exercise 8

CREATING YOUR OWN VISION BOOK/BOARD

1. Schedule a day and a time that you are going to give to yourself to create your vision book and stick to it. You deserve this time!

2. Gather magazines, pictures off the internet, inspirational quotes and affirmations.

3. You will need to buy yourself a scrapbook or a journal with blank pages. Find one that feels good to you when you look at it. You will also need scissors and glue.

4. On your chosen day and time, try and remove anything that may distract you, turn off the phone if possible and try and make sure you won't be disturbed. This is a very sacred and powerfully creative time between you and your dreams! Lighting candles, playing music that you connect with, and inspires you also helps. Gather all that you need whether on the floor or table. Get comfortable.

5. Just before I begin, I like to state my intention and say a little prayer, but you do not have to

do this. I begin by asking my angels and guides (pray to whoever and whatever feels right for you, Source, Spirit, Universe, God etc) to guide me in this process and help me to hear my dreams clearly, guide me to what is for my highest good and greatest joy and I finish by saying thank you as if it is already done!

6. Begin! Have fun! There is no right or wrong....

7. When you are finished look at your creation and thank yourself for giving this time to your dreams. Place the book by your bed or somewhere where you will look at it first thing in the morning and last thing at night. The more you look at it, the deeper it goes into the subconscious mind.

8. Now just watch the miracles happen! BELIEVE!

Day 9: Fuel for success

- Your body is the vehicle that carries you through the journey of your life

- The fuel you put in is critical to how effectively the vehicle functions.

- If the fuel is wrong you will feel the effects.

- Some of the effects of the wrong fuel are

    - Lack of energy

    - Stomach pains

    - Back pain

    - Weight issues

    - Headaches

    - Skin issues

    - IBS

    - Lower immune system

- Fuel comes from:

    - The thoughts we have- thoughts create energy, then feelings in the body and effect the cells in the body.

    - The food we eat

- Physical Activity
  - Sleep
- We can change the fuel to help us journey through life more effectively and optimally. Our fuel will determine how we feel every day and experience life.

Exercise 9

There are 3 parts to this exercise, FOOD, PHYSICAL ACTIVITY and SLEEP

Part A

FOOD:

- List 5 foods that you eat every day.

- If any of the 5 foods are: ALCOHOL, CAFFEINE, HIGHLY PROCESSED, FAST FOOD, HIGH SUGAR, WHITE BREAD, WHITE SUGAR, WHITE FLOUR AND WHITE RICE, then you may not be providing the optimum fuel for your body.

- Over the next week become aware of how you feel after eating any of the foods from the above list.

- Cut out one food from the above list for a week and notice if you feel any difference.

- Some super-foods for fuel and moods : WALNUTS, BANANA, YOGHURT, BRAZIL NUTS, AVOCADO, OILY FISH, CHIA SEEDS, COCONUT OIL, SPIRULINA, FLAXSEEDS

Part B

PHYSICAL ACTIVITY:

- Releases hormones that help the body and mind to feel good

- Benefits of 30mins of physical activity a day

- Improved sleep

- Boost immune system

- Decrease the risk of heart attack

- Lowers blood pressure

- Reduce risk of stroke

- Reduce back pain

- Boost self confidence

- Reduce stress

- Do something you enjoy

- Look at your current physical activity

- Write 1 goal regarding your physical health

- Write 1 action step

- Do it every day for at least 30 days

SLEEP

- Very important fuel

- We need to prioritise sleep. We tend to prioritise the "doing" and the "results" not the resting or relaxing.

- We have a "circadian rhythm", an internal biological clock that regulates the timing of sleeping and waking over 24hrs.

- Our strongest sleep drive usually occurs between 2-4am and 1-3pm

- The sleepiness we experience during these times will be more intense when we are sleep deprived or less intense if we had sufficient sleep.

- Teenagers strongest drive for sleep is 3-7am and 2-5pm

- A regular routine sleep cycle is vital for daily performance and to achieving our desired goals and life experiences.

- Effects of not getting enough sleep:

  - Weight gain

  - Increased stress and pain

  - Digestive problems

- Weakened immune system
- Mood imbalances
- Increased anxiety
- Hormonal imbalances
- Depression

- Optimum Sleep Cycle:
  - Go to bed and wake at the same time everyday
  - Outdoor exercise during the day
  - Last meal 3hrs before bed
  - Avoid nicotine and caffeine
  - Avoid TV/computer 30mins before sleep
  - Ensure room is dark, quiet, calm, optimum temp approximately 16-18 Celsius.
  - Use aromatherapy.
  - POWER 45MINS BEFORE BED (the subconscious mind replays the last 45mins before sleep 6 times more than any other time)
  - Meditate

- Review successes of the day
- Review goals, affirmations and visualisations
- Read an uplifting book
- Take an "ultra-bath" (2 cups Epsom salts, 1/2 cup baking soda, 10 drops lavender for 20mins)

- Look at your current sleep cycle

- Do you feel rested in the morning?

- Are there any changes you can make?

- Set 1 goal and begin today, try it for at least the duration of this workbook.

Day 10: What is our Spirit?

- Centre of who we are

- Unique to everybody

- Core of your being

- Eternal, never-ending

- Essence of who we are

- Highest most noble part of who we are

- Fingerprint of God that becomes the physical body

- Soul is connected to your purpose

- Carries all the messages and lessons that we have learnt

- Innermost being

- Consciousness beyond form

- Watches the mind

- Changeless part of us

- The truth of who we are

- Divine part of us

- Everybody has a spirit

- Non-physical part of the person

- The stillness separate from our thoughts

For some people, the word spirit implies religion, spirit is not religion. However if the word spirit is uncomfortable for you, find a word that feels comfortable to best describe the above. Some of the words that I have heard it described are, Source, God, Light, Divine being, Divine source, Universe, Universal energy, Creator, Truth and Divine Love. Find a word that is your connection to peace, calm, joy, happiness, contentment, connection, intuition and clarity. For this book I will use the word Spirit as this is what feels comfortable for me.

I believe that my spirit is my truest self, the most loving and authentic part of me. The energy that I was born with, the unconditional love that I knew coming into this world before I learnt what fear was. The part of me that is beyond my limiting beliefs, my fears and worries, my self-doubt and unworthiness. My spirit doesn't question my deserving of love, whether I am good enough or not, whether I am worthy of love. Spirit to me is pure love, joy, truth, acceptance and non-judgement. It is an authentic, wondrous, amazing, awesome and fun love that lives within and is there always. I can disconnect from that love and forget it is within, when I am in a fearful state of mind I am disconnected from my spirit. We disconnect regularly in this world, however we can learn how to find our way back to our truth, that cosy, warm, safe, nourishing and nurturing love anytime we want to. I often think of the movie, The Wizard of Oz and how Dorothy was lost and trying to find her way home, only to realise after going through quite a frightening journey that the power to go "home" had been with her all the time in the ruby slippers. We have the power to return to the home within us, our loving centre, anytime, we just need to know how to click the ruby slippers together! Throughout these pages I try and help you find *your* ruby slippers. Let us begin on the yellow brick road!

Michelangelo took a big chunk of marble and believed the statue was already inside the marble, he just had to get rid of the excess marble. *We* have to get rid of our excess marble which are our fears,
worries, limiting beliefs etc. to reveal our spirit, our truth.

- If you bring awareness to your spirit daily you will experience
    - Greater balance and flow in life
    - Greater clarity
    - Greater feeling of meaning and purpose
    - Greater connection to others

- Feelings of joy

- More passion

- Feel life has meaning

- Less vulnerable and alone

- More peace and calm

- Reduces stress and fear

- Increases feelings of wellbeing

- Balances the body and mind

- How do I connect with my spirit daily?

  - Stillness and silence are important.

  - It is more challenging to hear our spirit when the mind is full of chatter so we need to try and quieten the mind.

  - We are surrounded by internal noise, the mind chatter and external noise, televisions, radios, phones, screens, people and busyness.

  - If you want to hear your spirit you need to stop distracting yourself.

"Learn to listen to what your inner voice is telling you and your whole world changes" - Oprah

Exercise 10

- Connecting to the spirit takes silence

- 5 mins a day of meditation (we will look at mediation later on in this book) or intentionally focusing on our breath can really help connect us to the infinite wisdom within. Imagine having an all knowing, wise guide inside you 24 hours a day, always guiding you on the path that will bring you to the highest, most alive and joyful version of you.. what comfort would that bring into your life?

- Deep Belly Breathing

  - Breathing is one of the easiest and best therapeutic modalities

  - It is available to us always

  - Stimulates vagus nerve and parasympathetic nervous system

  - No cost

  - Relaxes body

  - Reduces stress

  - Boost immune system

  - Enhances wellbeing

  - No special equipment

- Can stop mental chatter

- Simple and effective

- 5 mins of belly breathing now

  - 1 hand on belly and the other on chest

  - Breathe and notice which hand rises the most.

  - We want it to be the belly that rises the most.

  - Focus on breathing into the hand on the belly.

  - As you inhale the belly rises, inhale for 4 counts

  - As you breathe out belly lowers, exhale for 6 counts

  - You can picture white light going into the belly

  - Do this for 5 mins every day and anytime you feel stressed/fear

Try this intentional breathing exercise every day and watch the internal and external peace that you receive. There are so many benefits of taking this time for you every day. It is a simple practice but the results are phenomenal. You will shift internal fear and stress and that in turn will shift external fear and stress. How you will first notice the effects of this daily breathing exercise, is when you notice yourself reacting differently to the stresses in your life, the stress will not totally embody you and knock you off course. You will be able to stay more centred and grounded. Stress is a part of life but how we respond to it will alter our experience and ultimately affect the outcome.

Day 11: What is intuition?

What is intuition, is a question I get asked repeatedly given that I have trained as an intuitive healer! Having the word "intuition" in my job title, kind of opens me up to those questions!! I have worked with thousands of clients, empowering them and helping them to connect to the love within, to their spirit, and in that process to then be able to access their intuition at any time, and to trust it, so they can take action from that space. I have found, that when we can access the intuitive voice within and be able to tap into the inner guidance system at any time, and especially in times of stress, it reduces the level of fear and worry in our lives. It is unfortunate that modern day society doesn't place value on learning how to connect internally to our truth and love, we have been taught to place value in everything outside of us. However, as we are getting more and more stressed, chasing the external things that we have been taught to value, we are chasing them desperately looking for peace, for happiness and joy, for clarity and connection but just like Dorothy in The Wizard of Oz, we need to start having the awareness that it has been inside us all along. We need to learn how to connect to the infinite wisdom and peace within on a daily basis. Connecting to your own intuition will empower, inspire and equip you to enjoy the adventure that life is!

Intuition is:

- An incredibly powerful and under-utilised part of ourselves

- It is a sensation that appears in the consciousness without us fully being aware of the underlying reasons for its occurrence.

- It is ability to know something without analytical reasoning

- It is the ability to "see" things our eyes cannot see and to "know" things that our thinking mind cannot know.

- When we get out of our thinking mind we can use our intuition to our greatest advantage.

- It is an inner wisdom that can guide us in all areas of our lives. It is our connection to the big picture!

- When we make decisions/choices using our intuition it feels safe, exciting rather than frightening, feels right without being able to explain why and can be at odds with the analytical mind which can make it challenging for us to trust.

- We find it difficult to trust, because it is a huge part of us, that we haven't learnt how to tap into and we also haven't learnt to value. We are taught to value the logical and analytical mind. If we can learn how to use all parts of us, the whole of us and value ourselves wholeheartedly, we will find balance and self-love.

- Our intuition is hooked up and connected to the universal radio waves/ universal awareness.

- Intuition comes from the right brain

- How to listen to your intuition?

  - Silence the mind (deep belly breathing from previous exercise helps with this)

  - Ask the universe to help you hear your intuition, by asking, "Where would you have me go? What would you have me do and What would you have me say and to whom?"

  - Listen to the whispers.

  - Don't force the whispers to come, just try and create the most hospitable environment for your intuition to speak to you. Get yourself into a state of being where you feel most calm, for example, deep breathing, in nature, in the bath, exercising, there is no right or wrong, it just makes it easier to hear your intuition when you can quieten your mind.

- Ask your angels, God, guides, universe, source to give you signs that you will recognise

- Practice, practice, practice

- We are receiving signals all the time, you just need to have an intention that you want to hear what your intuition has to say.

- Some people use angel cards to ask their intuition to give them the message through the card they pick. Before you meditate or do your belly breathing you can ask your spirit to let you be able to hear your intuition clearly.

"The intuitive mind is a sacred gift and the rational mind is a faithful servant. We have created a society that honours the servant and has forgotten the gift." Albert Einstein

Exercise 11

- Notice over the next week any gut feelings/ hunches/ inner whispers or guidance.

- Record them in a journal.

- Notice what you were doing when you felt or heard your intuition.

- Take note of how you feel when you hear your intuitive voice. Do you trust it? Do you doubt it? Do you feel nervous or excited?

You are now inviting your intuitive voice into your life and getting to know how it guides and inspires you. It is a daily practice that is so worth it!

Day 12: Building a relationship with your intuition

For most of us, our daily life is made up of making lots of decisions, some are small and some are big, life changing ones. These daily decisions can cause quite a lot of stress in our lives. Why does decision making cause so much stress? One word... FEAR!

FEAR is what makes decisions feel so stressful and uncomfortable for us.

What are we afraid of?

- Making the "wrong" decision
- Not getting it right and ultimately failing.
- We are frightened about what other people will think of our decision.
- Frightened of being rejected.
- Fear of the unknown and uncertainty
- Fear of not having control of the outcome.
- Fear of making a mistake
- Fear of not being perfect

These are only some of the fearful thoughts that come into our minds when we try to make decisions. We may not be aware of the individual fears when we are trying to make a decision, we may just feel frightened, and stuck about what option or path to choose. Stress builds internally, the more and more fear we let in, we will actually paralyse ourselves, that we can't make a decision at all and inevitably feel stuck. If we get so afraid to make a decision, we might look to others to make the decision for us. Getting someone else to make a decision for you, because the fear is so loud, actually completely disempowers you and doesn't allow your true strength and knowing to be revealed. If we can learn how to tune into our own intuition when decisions need to be made, we will feel peaceful and calm when making the decision. The decision will not be made from a place of fear, it will be made from a place of love. I believe, that making decisions from a place of love will never lead you down the wrong path.

In the previous exercise, you started to become aware and record your intuitive feelings, in this next exercise we will go deeper into your relationship with your intuition.

Exercise 12

- Journaling is one of the most effective ways to develop your intuition, to get to know what it sounds like to you and how it shows up in your daily life.

- A lot of people have fears about writing in a journal in case someone finds it and reads it. We want *this* journal to be unedited and not controlled by your fearful mind. If we are afraid what people would think if they read it, we will not write down our truth. Find a way of recording it, where you know it will be kept private. Some people choose to record on their computer, to dictate into a personal recorder or the good old diary! Choose whatever form feels most comfortable to you.

- Be aware of resistance and fearful thoughts that block you doing this exercise.

- Do it anyway, even though it is uncomfortable. Sometimes getting uncomfortable leads us to the biggest breakthroughs.

- Every morning when you wake, before you do anything else, reach for your journal and just write whatever comes to you. Write for as long as you feel is right for you. You will probably feel a naturally ending and conclusion, it will feel like you have released all that you need to. First thing in the morning is ideal, as our habitual, fearful thought patterns and beliefs haven't kicked in fully, so we will be able to hear our intuitive loving voice a little easier. However, if the morning doesn't work for your lifestyle, just do it whenever you feel drawn to it, but try and do it every day as the answers and insights will flow the more we practice.

- Journaling really helps to get the worries and fears out of our minds, and therefore we don't have to keep repeating the same thoughts over and over again. We gain more clarity and peace. As a daily practice, we are also inviting our intuition into our lives and setting the intention that we are willing to listen.

- Do your best to journal everyday so that it becomes part of your routine, but please don't judge yourself if you miss a day, this is not meant to be another thing you criticise or judge yourself harshly for. This exercise is about bringing more clarity, peace, joy, connection and love into your life, not another way to add to your list of things you aren't good enough at or didn't get done!

Day 13: Attitude of gratitude

Developing an attitude of gratitude, is one of the most transformational things you can do to bring more love, joy and happiness into your life. We can develop an attitude of gratitude, which, if practiced on a daily basis, will reduce fear and worry, bring feelings of happiness and contentment and also attract and manifest more things to be grateful for! It's a win win!

"Be thankful for what you have, you'll end up having more. If you concentrate on what you don't have, you will never ever have enough." – Oprah Winfrey

In the society that we live in at present, we are conditioned to believe we never have enough, or even worse, that *we* are never enough as human beings. Through advertising, the media and through the words and language we speak, for most of us, we feel like we are lacking something and that if we acquire the "thing" we are lacking, then we will be complete and happy. The "thing" we are lacking tends to be something outside of us, something external, a different job, a new car, a new relationship, a new home, different clothes and the list goes on.

By believing that we don't have enough, or that *we* aren't enough as we are, we are affirming to the

Universe, that we are not good enough or deserving enough to have happiness and love . As we have learnt earlier in this book, how we speak and what words we affirm create very powerful energy. If I am putting out a belief, that I am not enough or I don't have enough and I won't be happy until I have... then we manifest that same energy back and get more of the same feelings and outcomes.

To create more in your life, that you are grateful for, you must create the feeling of gratitude for what you already have. This is sending a very positive affirmation out into the universe and also into your subconscious mind. Gratitude for what we have sends a message that I AM deserving, I AM living a life that is filled with good. This then creates a vibration and energy within you that works on your subconscious mind and this in turn creates more of the same in your life. If you think and feel, all that is good in your life, however small it may seem, you create a momentum and a force that goes about creating more and more to be grateful for, this is to match the energy that you started to create.

Being grateful for the things in our life that make us happy, puts a focus on the things that are important to us, and our subconscious mind interprets this and goes about creating more of the same. Where thought goes, energy flows!

Gratitude is a miracle cure! Having an attitude of gratitude focuses our energy and thoughts on what is positive in our lives. What we think about and focus our energy on, is mirrored back to us, so therefore, if we focus on all that is good in our lives, we will see more good in our lives!

When we focus on lack, we create more feelings and evidence of lack in our lives.

When we focus on what we have that is good, we create feelings and evidence of abundance and good in our lives.

"As soon as you start to feel differently about what you already have, you will start to attract more of the good things, more of the things you can be grateful for." – Joe Vitale

When I become aware that I am feeling worried or fearful, I take a breath and list off all that I am grateful for in my life. I may resist doing this at first because my mind thinks that such a simple exercise couldn't possibly change the worry or fear that I am feeling, however I persevere and every time I am amazed and how quickly it shifts the worry and fear and how clearly I am able to think of a solution to what is bothering me. More importantly, in the moment, I actually feel calmer and happier and how I feel, makes such a difference to my day.

Creating an attitude of gratitude is a daily practice, but one, that I know transforms your daily energy, and in turn, your daily life.

"The grateful mind is constantly fixated upon the best. Therefore it tends to become the best. It takes the form or character from the best, and will receive the best." – Wallace D.Wattles

Exercise 13

CREATING AN ATTITUDE OF GRATITUDE

1. Buy a new journal, or, you can use the one you have been using for this workbook. I like to have a separate "gratitude journal", I have a small little one that I carry with me to record in and read when I need a lift!

2. Every night before you go asleep, write down 5 things you are grateful for on that day. It could be some kindness you received, your health, the food you ate, the nice message you received, your home, your warm bed, the morning cup of tea, whatever you feel was good about that day. On the days where we are struggling and life seems to not be going the way we want, it will be more of a challenge to find 5 things, but keep at it until you think of 5 things to be grateful for, even if it's just that you are still breathing!

3. Do this every day, and you will see the Universal energy, bring you more things to be grateful for. In fact, the more you do this exercise, you start finding more than 5 things to be grateful for and your lists get longer! How great would it be, to have a really long list of things to be grateful for!? How do you think this would make you feel on a daily basis?

Day 14: Stop "shoulding" all over yourself!!

As we have learnt, in our previous exercises, our thoughts and words have a very powerful effect on how we feel, which in turn effects how our day looks and feels to us, which then in turn effects what experiences we are manifesting.

Everything is connected, our thoughts that are created in our mind, create feelings in the body and these feelings will either lift us up or knock us down.

"Keep your thoughts positive, because your thoughts become your words. Keep your words positive, because your words become your behaviours. Keep your behaviours positive, because your behaviours become your habits. Keep your habits positive, because your habits become your values. Keep your values positive, because your values become your destiny." – Gandhi

We learn our words at a very early age, and that is how we learn to communicate what we are thinking and how we are feeling. Words allow us to communicate and connect with others. Our own words or somebody else's have the power to knock us down or lift us up. Don't underestimate the power, energy and meaning in our words.

In my work with clients around the world from different cultures and societies, I have seen how similar and connected we all are in so many ways. We have common beliefs, thoughts and words.

One of the ways we cause such stress and resistance in our minds and our bodies, is in the words we use, when talking to ourselves and to others. When we are speaking unkindly to someone else, it inevitably causes feelings of stress. When we are speaking to ourselves unkindly, through our thoughts and words it also causes feelings of stress.

One of the words I want to focus on, is the word "SHOULD".

When you say this word, does it feel uplifting or does it feel stressful and do you feel resistance?

For example, say aloud the following statements:

"I should have said that better"

"I shouldn't have said that"

"I should be thinner"

"I should lose weight and be fitter"

"I should be smarter and better"

The list could go on and on!

How did it feel when you read those statements aloud?

Uplifting and encouraging or stressful and worrying?

Do you ever say these statements aloud or to yourself? How often do you think you use the word "SHOULD" in a day? For most of us, the word "SHOULD" features heavily in our daily vocabulary.

The word "SHOULD" is basically telling yourself, at the deepest level of your being, that you, or the situation is not good enough, not right and not the way it is supposed to be. It is a total rejection of you, and the present moment. We are now closing ourselves off from seeing the good in ourselves or the situation we are referring to. It pushes us down and demotivates us, it lowers our energy and vibration and is unlikely to help us see the positive or loving solution.

What can we do to change this negative and harmful approach? We can simply, pick a different word when we are describing ourselves or the situation. We can't just remove a word without replacing it with something. However, a different word can create a totally different meaning, interpretation, energy and action. This is turn creates a very different experience, and we see a different response from those around us and within ourselves.

When you replace the word "SHOULD" with the word "COULD", you are giving yourself and the Universe a very different message. You are not rejecting what is and you are empowering yourself with a choice.

The word "COULD" acknowledges our inner strength and ability to make choices, to create how *we* want to be and we don't feel the resistance, like something outside of us is telling us how we have to be. When we feel pressured to be, act, think or feel a certain way, we tend to feel resistance and want to push against this. This creates internal stress in the body and mind.

The word "COULD" empowers us, uplifts us and motivates us to make choices that feel right and true for us as a unique individual.

Read the above statements again and replace the word "SHOULD" with "COULD". Do you feel any different? Do you notice a lighter feeling? Do you feel freer and less pressure? It is amazing the difference one word can make to how we feel, act, and to the response we get from others and the universe.

Exercise 14

STOP THE "SHOULDING"!

1. When you wake in the morning, ask your spirit to help you be aware of all the times you use the word "SHOULD" in your thoughts or words.

2. As you go through your day, when you become aware of a thought or statement that you used that contained the word "SHOULD", Stop, take a breath and replace the word "SHOULD" with "COULD".

3. Say out loud if possible, the new statement or thought, with the word "COULD" instead.

4. Notice how it feels, does it uplift you and feel less stressful?

5. At the end of the day, record in your journal 1 or 2 examples of this. Record what the thought or

statement was, the new thought or statement with the word "COULD" and the difference in how you felt when you removed the word "SHOULD".

6. Please don't use this exercise as a way to judge yourself by counting all the times you used the word "SHOULD". Don't criticise yourself for using "SHOULD". All you are doing, is becoming aware of a word that may not be serving you in the best possible way. Becoming aware is the first step in changing anything. If you judge yourself harshly, you are just amplifying the negative energy and making yourself feel even more demotivated and not good enough. Simply become aware, no judgement, and then take action by replacing "SHOULD" with "COULD". No need for judgements! You are just retraining your mind to help you, as you go through your daily life.

7. When changing anything, whether it is a thought, behaviour or habit, remember the 3 A'S! A for Awareness, A for Acceptance and A for Action. The first step is becoming AWARE of the thing we want to change. ACCEPTING that it is there with no judgement of ourselves and ACTION, when

we take an action from a place of acceptance, it is a positive and loving action that will bring us to whatever is for our highest good and greatest joy.

Day 15: Stillness Speaks

Life is busy. Life is "doing" lots and trying to get somewhere or get something. We have been taught to value ourselves when we are "doing" lots and really busy. It is like we are using the description of our lives being "so busy" as a badge of honour and a sign we are successful. Yes, "doing" and taking action is important but there is another piece of the puzzle that most of us are missing. A lot of the time, we are feeling like we are doing, doing, doing and getting nowhere fast. This feeling, is because we are missing the other piece that works side by side with the "doing".

What is the other piece of the puzzle? The answer, is to step into "being". To feel like we are moving forward, towards our dreams, and to see the results in our daily lives, we have to balance the "being" and the "doing".

What is "being"? There are many meanings to the word "being", but for this exercise, we are going to use it in the context of simply resting in the space of non-doing, of silence and stillness. It is like, pressing the pause button, taking a time out to be with you, pausing the chitter-chatter of the mind, not thinking about the past and the future and the judgements we are having about every moment of the day and ourselves.

To feel energised, inspired, peaceful, happy and calm in our day, it is so important to connect to our spirit, our true self, our inner voice, our intuition on a daily basis. To really listen to, and hear, what our inner guidance is trying to say to us, or not even to hear anything, to just connect to the calm within us, we must take time to be silent.

One of the difficulties we have in today's world, is getting time where we can be still and silent. We are so "connected" to outside sources, through television, internet, phones, radio and media. We think we are getting the whole story of what is going on, but there is a really powerful loving guidance system with lots of Inspiring information, just for you, and for your highest good that we are not hearing. It is desperately trying to get our attention, to help guide and nourish us, yet we choose not to listen or we just don't know how, because we were never taught and no value is placed on this information. It is trying to get us to hear, and yet we never take time to "connect" to it.

My life transformed when I started to listen and value what my spirit was saying. Trust me, when I started, I hadn't a clue what I was doing, no one had ever told me that there was this amazing, loving, wise guide inside of me, always looking out for my highest good. I could have saved myself a lot of suffering, if I had learnt how to listen to it earlier in life! I truly believe, that when we take time to value connecting with our true selves by being still and silent we will bring balance, wellbeing, happiness and wholeness into our lives.

So many of us, in today's world, are feeling out of control, lost, afraid, alone, disconnected, unfulfilled, uninspired, unwell, unbalanced and because of these feelings we are always searching outside ourselves for the answers. Of course, there is always help and support outside of you, once you ask, it can show up in your life but the greatest help you can give yourself, is when you connect with your true self, your spirit, the love inside. That is where you will find your answers, wisdom that will guide you, to take inspired actions every day.

Exercise 15

LETTING THE STILLNESS SPEAK TO YOU

1. Today you are going to gift yourself with time to be silent and still.

2. To your conditioned mind, that has learnt, that, only when I am *doing* something, I am of value, this exercise will probably bring up a lot of resistance.

3. Notice what resistant thoughts you are having; For example, "This is a waste of time", "I'm not actually doing anything", "I didn't see any results or changes straight away", "I can't sit still and be silent" "My mind doesn't stop thinking" "I don't have time to do this", "My life is too busy to do this", "I have 3 kids running around, I don't get any time to be still and silent". These thoughts may seem very valid to you right now and I am not saying they are not real, all I ask, is that you remember the H.O.W. So when your mind thinks, "How can I feel better, calmer and happier in my day?" you remember the H.O.W. I must be honest, open and willing. Just be willing to try something that you may not have tried

before. Just be open. I know that it is challenging, but when you just stay willing, even when the mind is resisting, you will in time, be so glad you gave yourself the gift of this daily practice. Also, everyone around you, from your kids, your partner, your friends, your co-workers and family, will be really happy that you gave yourself this silent time because your energy, kindness, love and connection will be strengthened.

4. Pick a time today, maybe when you normally would be on the computer, watching TV or reading and instead, disconnect from everything outside and reconnect to everything inside.

5. Put a timer on somewhere, maybe your phone or a clock, set it for 5mins if possible, if you can only do a minute, that's great too. Just stop everything and breathe. You don't have to breathe in any special way, this is just a time to reconnect. No fancy equipment required!

"Listen to what your inner voice is telling you and your whole world changes" - Oprah

Day 16: Meditation for daily living

When I mention the word, "meditation" at any of my workshops or courses, I can visibly see the discomfort and fear in people. We have so many preconceived judgements and beliefs about meditation, and many images pop into our head when we think of it. We think that mediation, is something only really spiritual people can do, we picture the guy wearing the robes with long hair sitting on a cushion for hours, we think our minds can't be still and sit for long, we think that we can't do it, and it is only for a certain type of person. I have heard all the arguments against mediation and all the resistance. When I first attempted meditation, I was definitely a resister. I had a fear of failing, I always wanted to get things perfectly right, I just couldn't allow myself do something that I thought I couldn't do perfectly. I know that many people feel this way about meditation and stop themselves even trying. The ironic thing is, that meditation actually allows you to be comfortable with imperfection.

Eventually, and thankfully, many years ago, after reading about the benefits of mediation everywhere I allowed myself to try it! Every book I read, talked about the benefits of meditation, every teacher I had, told me how much I would benefit from it so after much procrastination I took the first step.... The first step was committing to 3 minutes a day of meditation!! Yes, I started with 3 minutes, small steps in the direction of where you want to go become giant leaps in time. It wasn't easy to get on the cushion. I had to get a special cushion, and get everything set up perfectly to play the part of the expert meditator! You really don't need anything at all, except willingness and openness to a new experience.

Creating a daily meditation practice has truly transformed my life and the lives of thousands of my clients. Not everyone likes to meditate, and it is definitely not about feeling that, you "SHOULD" do it, however, if you are looking to feel, calm, peace, joy, happiness, connection and balance, it is definitely going to help you to cultivate those feelings daily.

There are so many books about mediation, listing all the health benefits, so if you would like to know more, just type the word, "meditation" into the search engine on your computer, and you will have more information than you could know what to do with. I know, that when I first started to learn about all the benefits of meditation, I started to feel guilty that I wasn't doing it, as all the experts were doing it, and what was wrong with me that I couldn't do it!! As we learnt in the earlier exercises, the word "should" just creates resistance, the more you say "should", the more you will resist it. Once I decided that /wanted to try it and it was my choice, I became open and willing to try. So, I don't want to list off all the benefits, here in this workbook, in case you get the same attack of the "guilts" and the "shoulds"!!

Let me just say, that it is worth a try, you have nothing to lose and so much to gain, it is free, you need no fancy equipment, it is something you can carry with you wherever you go and it is a habit that you can cling to when times are tough. It has been my rescuer in this journey of life, many times over and continues to be one of my daily essentials.

For those of you, who possibly already have a strong daily meditation practice, it is no harm to remind yourself of the basics and to also notice any resistance you may have to giving yourself the time to practice something that you obviously enjoy.

Become aware of the resistance to give ourselves time every day, that is just for us and our wellbeing.

Meditation is a practice. Some days you will feel, were better than others, I try and not analyse or judge my mediation time, there is no good or bad mediation. Showing up is all that counts! 90% of the practice of creating new habits, is just showing up!

There are so many different ways to meditate, and you will, in time find what works for you, you might try different mediations at different times in your life, as I said, there is no right or wrong.

I like using a 'mantra", as it helps my mind to be quiet, and also the vibration of the mantra deepens my connection. Mantras are Sanskrit syllables and can be viewed as ancient power words with intentions that help us connect to spirit. "OM" is a mantra that some of you may be aware of, it represents the infinite universal consciousness and some people like to meditate repeating "OM" quietly in their minds.

There are also guided mediations, where you listen to a recording of someone guiding you through the mediation and many people find this helpful when they are trying meditation for the first time. There is also silent meditation, just focusing on the breath and maybe counting the breaths as they inhale and exhale. There are countless versions and variations to meditation, as I said, there is no right or wrong mediation. You can try as many versions as you like, as long, as you are trying to create a daily practice and committing to giving this time to you, you will feel a difference in your day to day life, whatever that looks like.

"Prayer is talking to God. Mediation is letting God talk to you" - Yogi Bhajan

Exercise 16

<u>YES YOU CAN MEDITATE!</u>

1. Decide a time today that you are going to give 5 minutes of your day to meditate.

2. When the time comes, turn off all phones and try and limit any distractions. Put a timer on, set to go off after 5 minutes.

3. Sit comfortably. You can sit in whatever position is comfortable for you, with your legs crossed on the floor, or on a straight back chair with your feet on the floor and hands resting on your legs, these are two of the most common positions but again decide what feels right for you. Try not to meditate lying down or you may just fall asleep!

4. Lightly close your eyes. Relax your shoulders and rest your hands on your thighs. I like to touch my thumb and first finger together and place my palms facing up but that is just what works for me!

5. Take a few long, slow, deep, belly breaths.

6. After you have taken a few of these breaths, let your breathing fall into a natural rhythm.

7. For this meditation, on the inhale, quietly in your mind, say "Calm body". On the exhale, quietly in your

mind, say "Calm mind". Repeat these phrases as you inhale and exhale.

8. Your mind will wander and start thinking of what you have to do afterwards, what you want to eat later, random thoughts, one thing is for sure, it will wander! Please don't judge or criticise yourself if it does, you are not getting it wrong, as soon as you notice your mind has wandered, just go back to repeating the phrase.

9. Continue this until the timer goes off, when it does just take a moment or two to take a few big, deep belly breaths and then open your eyes and you are ready to go. You have connected to your spirit, your inner truth, your inner guide, to the love within. All the answers are in there for you.

10. You can do only 5 minutes a day, if that is what works for you. Or you can gradually increase the time if you feel guided to. The most important thing is to make sure it is consistent. If you want to see, and feel the results, which we all want to get, when we do anything, then you must do it consistently.

"The miracle comes quietly into the mind that stops an instant and is still" - A Course in Miracles

Day 17: Money worries – how to change the script!

Worry, we all do it! To me, I see worry like a virus. Our minds seem to pick the virus up when we least expect it, and once it gets in, it can take us over, and we become a victim and hostage to the worry virus. It can really cause a lot of stress and illness in the body and mind on a daily basis.

At the root of worry, is FEAR. We are frightened about something happening or not happening in the future or fearful of something from the past. When we are worrying, we are not in the present moment, we are in the future or in the past. In this workbook, we have looked at ways of bringing us back to the present moment, and therefore reducing or eliminating the fear and worry in the body and mind. We have looked at identifying fearful beliefs and thoughts, and turning them into positive affirmations, this turns down the volume on the worry or stops the worry virus coming into your mind and body. We have also looked at deep breathing, and mediation, these help hugely to bring us back to the present moment and to build our "emotional immune system" so we won't get so easily infected by the worry virus. When we practice the exercises daily, even on the days when we are not infected by the worry virus, then, when we do get attacked by the virus, we are able to heal and pass through the "infection" more peacefully and more quickly.

One of the major causes of worry for people in society today, is, MONEY. Money worries are attacking and infecting people globally, it is an epidemic and a virus that has spread viciously over the last years, with the global economic recession. The fear of money and the lack of it, has paralysed people from moving forward, it seems to have robbed people of their happiness and joy. The level of worry is preventing any changes to the situation.

I am certainly not going to solve the economic crisis here in this workbook, nor am I saying that money worries aren't real or valid, I am simply offering a way, to help clear the virus and give you some relief and peace. I know that money is a complex energy. Money is energy. We have attached so many judgements and beliefs to money, that it has become a very detailed and complex energy. I could write a whole book on money alone, so for this workbook, I want to give you a few simple tools, that may help lift some of the despair, worry and fear around money and abundance. Regardless of your money situation, we could all do with a little clearing out of any worries and fears we may have around the subject of money and abundance. I have yet to come across someone who doesn't have some worry, fear or block to money and abundance.

As money is a complex energy, that contains many many different layers, I am going to offer a few different exercises in the daily exercise section. My advice is to do them all, so you are giving the "money worry virus" a good clearing out!

Exercise 17

CLEARING THE MONEY WORRY VIRUS!

Part A

1. Write down all your fears about money in your journal.

2. Using the exercises that we did previously in this workbook on affirmations, create some positive affirmations that are the opposite of your fears. For example; **Fear** - "I can't pay my bills" **Affirmation** - "I AM paying all my bills with ease and money is flowing". I know, you will not believe this when you say it first because the current reality may be very different. However, we must change our thoughts to match our desire and the reality will then change. Thoughts first, reality second!

3. Repeat your positive money affirmations everyday, morning and night and then anytime you are aware that you are worrying or frightened about money.

Part B

1. Say an abundance prayer/request/intention every day.

2. The abundance prayer that I use, is as follows, but feel free to create your own: *"Thank you God for all the blessings in my life. Thank you for all the love and abundance. Thank you for helping me to create a healthy loving relationship to money. I know that I have fearful thoughts and beliefs around obey and abundance and I am ready to release them now. I ask that you take the thoughts and beliefs that are blocking money and abundance in my life. I hand them over to You. I welcome and am open to receive love and abundance in unexpected ways and in any way You wish to give it to me. I will pay attention to the guidance I receive. I am free from financial fear."*

3. Every time you pay a bill thank the universe/God/Source for giving you the ability to pay. When I pay for something in a store, online or a bill, I say a silent prayer as follows: *"Thank you God for giving me the ability and resources to be able to pay this bill and I give it with love"* Try it, and see how it changes how you feel towards letting money go.

<u>Part C</u>

1. To create true abundance in our lives, we need to look inside ourselves first, and see what beliefs we have, that may be blocking it from showing up.

2. Whatever we think about money, will create how we feel about money, and then how we will act around money. Thoughts create feelings, which in turn create actions.

3. Look at the fears you wrote down in exercise A and ask yourself what beliefs you have about money. Some of the most common beliefs we have, that block abundance are: The belief that there will never be enough for you, the belief that having a certain amount of money will make you more loved by people or better than you are now, or better than them, the belief that there is not enough to go around and so I have to compete with everyone else, the belief that it is not possible for you to have the money you desire and the belief that only certain people get to have financial freedom. We are also influenced by the media and news reports that instil a sense of fear in us about what is possible

with regards to the economy and money. Get honest with the beliefs you have and write them in your journal.

"Let's start with what we can be thankful for, and get our mind into that vibration, and then watch the good that starts to come, because one thought leads to another thought." – Bob Proctor

4. Forgive yourself for having those beliefs, don't judge yourself, you have learnt the fearful beliefs, you also can unlearn them and put in new ones. Say out loud, "I forgive myself for having these fearful beliefs around money and abundance, I release and let them go now".

5. When we are in a state of mind that is fearful about our finances, we tend to focus on what we don't have and what we can't afford, this creates more lack energy and more feelings of fear, which then attracts more of the same energy to you. To shift this energy and get a different outcome, we need to put the thoughts in, which will create a more positive result. Instead of focusing on all the things you don't have, write down in your journal all the things you do have. I know this is difficult when we are in a very

fearful place, but the only way to shift the fear is to get our mind to shift its perspective, and then we mirror that energy back to us. We need to clean out our fearful money beliefs, before we try and change anything on the outside.

"You cannot solve a problem in the same frequency in which it was created." – Lynn Grabhorn

Day 18: Decisions, decisions, decisions!

What I see, in my practice of working with my clients, and what I see in my own life, is how decision making, can cause such stress, confusion and fear. For a lot of people, decision making can bring stress and worry on a daily basis and this in turn creates a lot of ill-health and the feelings of being "stuck". The one thing we can be sure of in life, is that, we will be faced with having to make decisions. If decision making causes you a lot of fear and worry, then this is something that can suck the fun and joy out of your daily life. We are faced with the decisions from the time we wake until we sleep, even what time we will get out of bed is a decision. That is why, setting up daily routines and habits, gives us more time to focus on the decisions that may require more energy. If every day, we had to make decisions on what time we will get up, whether to brush our teeth or not, what to eat and so on, we would be using up a huge amount of energy and feel like everything is an effort. Having some things that we don't have to make a conscious decision about on a daily basis is very helpful.

There are decisions that will require our conscious attention and focus and it is important that we give them our time and energy, to make sure we are making decisions that are aligned with our truth. These decisions tend to cause the greatest stress as we know deep down that they are important to us. Fear and worry starts to come into our awareness, because we know they are important decisions and so therefore our fearful beliefs about ourselves and our lives tend to get triggered.

We all have fears, just as we all have love. There is no need to judge yourself for having fears, or if you find decision making a challenge. What makes decision making challenging and sometimes paralysing, is fear. Sometimes we will be aware of what we are frightened of or worried about, but very often the fears are subconscious and we are not so aware. To help with decision making, we need to become aware of the underlying and subconscious beliefs that are causing the fears, they are the root, and if we pull them out, the other fears tend to decrease or go completely.

What are your fearful beliefs around decision making?

The most common beliefs are; I am frightened that I will be rejected, I am frightened that I will make a mistake, I am frightened that people will judge me negatively, I am frightened of what people will think, I am frightened in case it all goes wrong, I am frightened that I am not good enough, I am frightened that I am not worthy of it all going great, I am frightened that I will fail, I am frightened that people won't approve, I am frightened of being wrong and sometimes, it is even, I am frightened of being a success and then losing it all, I am frightened of being a success and people treating me differently. As you were reading through those fears, you may identify with some of them, these are the fearful beliefs that are running through your subconscious mind, and are triggered, every time you have to make a decision. So, if we can change these beliefs, we will not be triggered and we can make decisions from a place of love and we will be able to hear our own inner guide, our intuition.

We looked at intuition in our earlier exercises, and how fear blocks us, being able to connect to it. We have looked at ways we can help ourselves, hear our inner voice. Being able to hear our intuition and inner guide, is really important when it comes to making decisions because we will make a decision that we believe in, feels right to us and we can invest in. We also won't be so effected by other people's opinions. The ideal way to make a decision is from a place of intuition and inner power, not fear. Let us now look at, how we can make decision making less fearful therefore easing our daily stress levels.

Exercise 18

DECISION MAKING IS FUN!

Part A

1. When I am faced with a decision, that I need to give attention and energy to, I set an intention - that I am going to listen and give the decision the time it deserves. I set aside time to focus on the decision in a conscious way. I try and get focused, because if I leave it unsupervised in my own mind, fear and worry may grab a hold of it and have a worry party!

2. In your journal write down the decision that needs your attention right now in your life. The say aloud or silently *"Dear God/ Universe/ Spirit please allow me to hear my intuition, my truth, clearly now. Please help me to see the signs and messages internally and externally that will guide me as I make this decision. Please help to see clearly the fears, worries and beliefs that are blocking me from hearing my truth about this situation. I release all fears and worries to you now and I trust in myself that I will make the decision that is for my highest good and*

greatest joy and all involved. Thank you God and so it is."

3. Now, let your pen guide you to write down all your fears and worries around the decision, for example; "I am frightened that I will make the wrong decision", "I am frightened that it won't work out the way I want it to", "I don't know what the right decision is for me", "I am worried that my partner won't approve" and "I am worried that I will make a mistake". Just let the fears and the worries flow out of you. Take as long as you need with this part. Get honest with yourself. It is like you are doing a deep cleaning on the inside to make room for what needs to come. We are cleaning out the fears so we can make room for the inspiration to pop into your awareness. Making inspired decisions always leads you on the path that is meant for your highest good.

4. Once you have your list of worries and fears, you are now going to release them out into the Universe, hand them over to God, the angels or to the Universal Higher Intelligence, whatever you feel comfortable with. We are now going to ask for help, and once we ask, it is given. We

must remember to ask. There is an intelligence that is greater and clearer than our fearful mind, so why not ask for help from that? We do not need to do everything on our own. Say out loud or silently; *"Universe, Angels, God, I ask you to take these fears and worries and to transform them into love, release them from me now so I am clean and clear and open to receive the highest, most loving, truthful guidance from within. Thank you God and so it is."* Some people like to burn the fear list, as they say the prayer. You can tear it up and throw it away or you can leave it in your journal as a reminder of the process and the courage you showed in acknowledging your fears.

5. Once you have done this, I encourage you to sit silently for 5-10 minutes and focus on your breath. You are now creating a space where inspiration, Divine guidance, universal energy and your intuition can speak to you. All you need to do, is focus on your breath, don't try and hear the answers, they will gently pop into your awareness.

6. When you have spent 5 or 10 minutes in silence, take a pen and your journal and let the

pen guide you, just write whatever comes to you, it may not make sense at the time but I guarantee the answers are in there and will come into your awareness. The more you do this practice, the easier it is to hear the answers.

Part B

1. Sometimes, we have to make decisions quickly and don't have time to go through the above process. When I need to make a decision quickly and am finding it difficult to hear my intuition, I will use one of these techniques, I will muscle test, use a pendulum or coin toss.

2. The body doesn't lie to us. Every muscle in the body either resists a decision or flows with it. Your mind will play tricks on you but your body never will. You can muscle test with a decision. The more you do this, the more you trust your body.

3. Select your question; "Should I purchase this red car?"

4. Rephrase the question as if you have already made the decision; "Yes I want to buy the red car"

5. Press the tip of your left thumb and little finger together. Put the top of the right thumb and index finger together, and link them into the opening created by the left thumb and little finger. Then pull the right thumb and index finger against the fingers of the left hand. If the O separates easily it means the choice feels weak for you and the body doesn't support it. This means it is a NO. If the fingers stay tight together, the choice feels strong to you, the body supports it so it is a YES.

6. The fearful mind may resist the messages you are getting but your body will not. The more you use this technique, the more you learn to listen and trust your body.

Part C

1. I also use a pendulum when making decisions. When you buy a crystal pendulum, clear the energy in it, by leaving it in salt water overnight and then rinse it off with clean water. Hold the crystal in your hand and ask spirit to infuse it with love and for it to be your guide, always guiding you to what is for your highest good.

2. When you need to make a decision, write out the question that it can be answered as a yes or no, for example; "It is right for me to go to the party tonight?" Hold the pendulum in your hand, close your eyes, take a few deep breaths to connect to your own intuition and spirit and then allow the pendulum to move. I interpret, that if it swings clockwise, that that is a YES and anti-clockwise is a NO. The more you use this technique, the more trusting and confident you will be in your intuition.

Part D

1. When I am really needing a quick decision on something, I will often do a "coin toss"! This can help us tune into what our gut and intuition is really trying to tell us.

2. Think of the decision. Decide what heads and tails will be, for example, heads is "I send the email" and tails is, "I don't send the email".

3. Toss the coin and notice your gut feeling when it lands. If you are disappointed or excited, it is telling you your true feeling.

4. Trust that your gut feeling is your own inner truth, your intuition, this is what is trying to speak to us underneath our fears.

Day 19: Everyday kindness

"This is my simple religion. There is no need for temples; no need for complicated philosophy. Our own brain, our own heart is our temple; the philosophy is kindness." - Dalai Lama

We are taught from a very young age that being kind is good. We are taught to share and to be nice to other children. We then start to move through life and go through challenges, painful times and more than likely, we are hurt and let down by people. What happens to us inside, when we go through these times? I believe, as we grow up, we start to get more and more afraid of life as we learn more about what can go wrong and how people can hurt us. As a result of fearing life more, we start to be afraid to give love out in case we don't get it back or we get hurt in the process. We retreat more into ourselves and start forming beliefs about how we need to be around others and we start getting suspicious of people's kindness and niceness. This breaks down and blocks the flow of giving and receiving kindness and love.

Even though we learn that it is more and more risky to be nice and kind in case we get hurt or experience pain, ironically the thing we are wanting and desiring is kindness and love. This sets up a vicious cycle, holding back our love and kindness in fear, waiting for it to come to us first before we give it out. As we have learnt through the exercises in this book, is that, we need to create the thoughts, feelings and actions that support and are in alignment with what we want to create. So, if we want to experience more loving kindness from others and within ourselves then we need to create thoughts, feelings and actions that support that wish, in order to manifest the same energy back to us.

What does all that mean in reality and in our daily lives? WE, have to be kind and loving in our thoughts and actions on a daily basis, to then see and feel loving kindness in our reality. You must give out, that which you wish to receive.

Most of us have probably heard the quote from the Bible,

"Do to others as you would have them do to you." Do to others as you would have them do to you.

Scientific studies are proving more and more, that when we give to others and show kindness that are levels of serotonin (the happy hormone) rises and our cortisol (the stress hormone) drops. The fact that it helps us physiologically is a bonus, because we actually feel the joy and happiness when we are kind to someone, instantly. When we are being kind, we are in our true self, perfect alignment, we are being what we are meant to be, we are living our purpose. We feel it in our gut, we can't logically explain why it makes us feel so good, we just know deep within us, the giving and kindness makes us feel like we make a difference. When we see that we have contributed to someone else's life, in a positive way, we feel a deep connection to something greater and feel like we have a purpose on this earth.

If being kind to others creates such joy, gives us so much connection and has so many health benefits, why do you not do it more often? We are afraid. What are we afraid of? We are afraid of being rejected, being hurt, being taken advantage of, being used, interfering in others' lives, being seen as silly, people looking at us suspiciously, what others will think and not seeing it returned. We have learnt all this fear. It is a heavy burden to carry and blocks so much love and abundance coming to us. I am not saying, you give and give, and sacrifice yourself, we can create healthy boundaries around giving. The healthy boundaries are created when we not only practice kindness for others, but also for ourselves. When we are giving and sacrificing ourselves in the process, we are not actually being kind to ourselves and therefore it really isn't a healthy kind energy, we are probably doing it because we feel we "should". Earlier on in this book, we looked at the problem with the word "should" and how much fear and resistance it creates. For it to be true kindness, it needs to work both ways, being kind to ourselves and to others. You may need to check in with yourself before you perform an act of kindness, and ask yourself, "Am I doing this because I truly want to or because I feel I should?" If it is not feeling like it is coming from your truth of really wanting to, you may be sacrificing yourself, which is not true kindness energy and so kind energy may not flow back.

Try to be kind without an expectation of needing to get it back, when we are sending out kind, loving energy, it will come back, not always directly at that time or in the way we expect but it does make its way back to you.

I could write a whole book on kindness and the benefits of performing acts of kindness, suffice to say, that the more you act from a state of kindness and love towards yourself and others, you will see more loving, kindness in your life. There have been many campaigns on the internet about performing random acts of kindness and it has spread so quickly because of the feel good factor it brings to us all. Try it, truly you have nothing to lose but your fears, and everything to gain. The more you are kind in your thoughts, words and actions, to yourself and others, fear simply dissolves!

Exercise 19

DAILY ACTS OF KINDNESS

1. Perform a random act of kindness to someone you love today. Do something kind that you don't normally do and that they weren't expecting. For example; send a loving message, call them out of the blue to tell them how much you appreciate them, cook a meal, put a love note in their lunch, put a love note under their pillow or take out the bins even if it's not your turn! Record in your journal what this experience was like, what you did, and how it felt. *"Do ordinary things with extraordinary love"* - St Therese of Lisieux.

2. Perform a random act of kindness towards yourself. This is a little more challenging, as it can trigger a lot of fear and guilt beliefs within us. Do something for yourself today that makes you happy and that you don't normally do. For example; Sit down for an extra 20 minutes and really let yourself enjoy

your morning coffee, have a luxurious bath, give yourself time to read your book, treat yourself to something that you normally would only do on a special occasion or simply don't do something that you feel you should do. Record in your journal what this experience was like, what you did and how you felt and what, or if any resistance showed up.

3. Perform a random act of kindness towards a stranger. This can be the most challenging for some as it may trigger fears of rejection and fears of what others will think. There are so many opportunities to be kind to others; for example, helping someone carry their shopping bags, offer to pay for their coffee, leave money at the till and ask the clerk to use it towards someone later, smile and say hello, give a thank you note to the person serving you in the store, tell someone how great a job they are doing and how good they are at their job. A simple smile and an acknowledgement can make such a

difference to someone's day. Never underestimate the power of kindness, it has a ripple effect. If there was tidal wave of kindness around the world and we all made it a priority, how different would this world be?

Day 20: Daily mindfulness

Mindfulness is coming into more and more people's awareness, and thankfully getting into places that it is really needed, like prisons and schools. It is not a new practice, it has been around for thousands of years, what is new, is that, the number of people that are being made aware of what mindfulness is, is increasing. It is also a practice that is being seen as accessible to all. What exactly is it? Mindfulness is being fully aware of the present moment with no judgement. Mindfulness means deliberately paying attention, being fully aware of what is happening in your body, mind and spirit and outside yourself in your environment. Mindfulness is awareness without judgement or criticism. When we are mindful, we are not comparing or judging the present moment. Anyone can do it and it changes everything!

"Few of us ever live in the present. We are forever anticipating what is to come or remembering what has gone." - Louis L'Amour

Most of us, in our daily lives get lost in thoughts about the past and the future, which tends to cause anxiety, worry and fear. This is a waste of our mental, emotional and physical energy. When we allow the mind to rest in the present moment, fully aware of the present moment, stopping the mind from going into the past and the future, we are conserving energy and feel energised daily.

"The best way to capture moments is to pay attention. This is how we cultivate mindfulness. Mindfulness means being awake. It means knowing what you are doing." — Jon Kabat-Zinn,

Mindfulness, like meditation, is a practice. Of course, the mind will wander, and go off into the future and the past but if we are consciously trying to be mindful, as soon as we notice our mind is wandering away from the present moment, don't judge it, just bring your awareness back to the present moment and focusing on your breath is great way to do that. Mindfulness is a simple but transformational practice. Mindfulness brings more meaning and enjoyment to the everyday activities that we do, taking care of the house, washing the dishes, your daily work, playing sport, raising children, and so on.

"Be happy in the moment, that's enough. Each moment is all we need, not more." - Mother Teresa

Our lives are made up of moments, and for most of us, we are so busy trying to reach the "destination" we are missing the moments. Life is the moments. There is nowhere to get to. This is it. This is the miracle. You are living it daily. Practicing mindfulness brings joy and curiosity into the everyday moments, the moments that we thought of, as boring or annoying, the judgements go and we become curious about life and the possibility each moment can bring. Mindfulness brings curiosity and when we are curious we are not judging, what we find, by being curious, is that life opens up, we see more possibility. If we see more possibility, our old beliefs that limit us, start to disappear and we start to take actions that feel more joyous and free. Whatever you are doing, whoever you are with, be fully present, it is the greatest gift you can give yourself and others.

Let us now look at something we do every day and how we can do it mindfully.

Exercise 20

<u>MINDFUL EATING</u>

Do you always eat in front of the television?

Do you always eat on the go?

Are you always in a rush when you are eating?

Do you always read while you are eating?

Are you aware of how you are feeling when you are eating?

Are you aware if you are feeling full or not?

If you are eating without being mindful, you are unaware of your bodies' messages and may ending up eating more than you really wanted to. We also miss all the enjoyment that food can bring because we are not using all of our senses. The distractions don't allow us to fully experience and enjoy our food.

1. Pick one mealtime today that you are going to practice mindful eating. It could be

breakfast, lunch, dinner or a snack time. It might be easier to start with a meal where you are alone if possible.

2. Try and remove all distractions. Turn off phones, computers, television and so on.

3. Take a few deep belly breaths before you begin to eat.

4. Look at your food and think of all the things that had to happen to get that food on your plate. Think of the farmers, the producers, the people that prepared it to be delivered to the store, the store workers, your energy and money that bought it, the energy required to prepare it and have it ready for you to eat. Thinking this way brings more gratitude and appreciation for the food we have.

5. Smell your food, look the shape and detail in the food.

6. Take a small bite, notice how it feels in your mouth.

7. Chew slowly and notice the texture of the food and the taste.

8. As you swallow, notice how it feels moving through and into your stomach.

9. Pay attention to how your body is feeling and when you are feeling full, listen and stop.

10. Take some deep breaths at the end of this exercise and congratulate yourself for eating with mindfulness and gratitude.

11. Record in your journal what this experience felt like. Did you notice your mind wandering? Did you notice much resistance to doing this exercise? Record it all with no judgement of yourself. You can do no wrong with this so there is no need for judgement.

"When walking, walk. When eating, eat" - Zen Proverb

Day 21: Ask for help

"Learning is the beginning of wealth. Learning is the beginning of health. Learning is the beginning of spirituality. Searching and learning is where the miracle process all begins." - Jim Rohn

I couldn't finish this book without giving time and attention to what I have been referring to throughout this workbook, and that is, the higher intelligence, the universal and divine energy, the spirit, the connection to something greater. This is not about religious beliefs, this is nothing to do with religion. This is about what is available to everyone and what I believe connects us all. I know, that for some people, when we use the words above, it can trigger a lot of judgement and beliefs about what is right and wrong. I definitely am not here to judge, and cannot, and will not, tell you what is right for you. I choose to live a spiritual life and practice living from this place every day.

Spirituality to me, is an awareness, that we are all connected to each other by a power or an energy greater than all of us, and that our connection to that power and to each other is founded in love and compassion. Spirituality gives me perspective, meaning and purpose. On a daily basis, my beliefs help me through the challenges and when pain shows up, I know that I am not alone. I have faced some major life challenges and had many dark nights of the soul, I know, that it has been my connection to my spirit and to the Divine energy that has helped me through, not only has it helped me to keep going, it has given me hope, resilience and a want, to take the pain and turn it into wisdom to help others.

"Spirituality is meant to take us beyond our tribal identity into a domain of awareness that is more universal." - Deepak Chopra

When I am connecting to the highest, most loving, universal energy I use the words, angels, God, guides, spirit and universe. They are words that resonate with me. I encourage you, as I did earlier in this book, to find words that resonate and feel right for you. Find something to connect with, outside of yourself. I believe, I have guides and angelic loving beings, helping me and looking out for me on a daily basis, even when I don't feel the connection or am doubting them, they are there. In the book about my life story, you will see how I have been rescued by my angels and how they keep producing miracles upon miracles in my life. They bring magic, fun, joy, comfort, love, compassion and a whole load of kindness. I wasn't always a believer, oh no, I was a complete sceptic and if you had told me 20 years ago that I would be writing a book and talking about angels and miracles, I most certainly would have laughed out loud! I needed clear signs to believe, I asked for the signs when I really needed them and I got them. We have to ask for the help, we have free will, and nothing can interfere in our life without our permission.

Many of my clients ask me how they can connect to their spirit, angels and guides. I simply respond with the word, ASK! You don't have to get down on your knees, say a special prayer, do a funny dance or ritual, you just have to ask as you would a friend. Your spirit is heard, listened to, the energy is sent out into the universal loving energy and sent back to you. I sometimes like to think of it, as sending our requests out into an airwave and it getting picked up by our angels and guides and sent back to us in the form of a message, a sign, through a person or simply, a feeling of comfort, love, peace and calm. You can ask a specific angel, guide, angelic, loving being, God, Buddha and so on or you can be general with the words, Source, Universe, Spirit, there is no right and wrong. There is only what is right for you. I really encourage you to find that connection to Love and ask, ask, ask. Ask for help, ask for guidance, ask for whatever you need, you are not being greedy, selfish or rude by asking, you are connecting to love, to bring more love into your life. How would the world look if there was more love?

Exercise 21

CONNECTING AND ASKING

1. Spend some time discovering what your spirit means to you. Give yourself time to read about and discover what energy, and help, may be there for you and what resonates with you.

2. Write out your thoughts and fears about your sprit in your journal. The answers normally show up in your words.

3. Find something that resonates and creates the vibration of unconditional love to you. Give it a name.

4. Start to build a relationship with this loving energy. Talk to it as you would a loved one.

5. ASK for help. ASK to see signs that you are being listened to. ASK to be open to receive the signs, guidance and messages.

6. Be patient and watch the miracles unfold.

The love is there for you. You are worthy and deserving. We are all connected by love. We are love. I AM LOVE.

"Whether you've seen angels floating around your bedroom or just found a ray of hope at a lonely moment, choosing to believe that something unseen is caring for you can be a life-shifting exercise." - Martha Beck

Final thoughts and wishes

Now you have completed the 21 day journey with me, I hope you have sensed and felt what my intentions were for this workbook. Every word, I can promise you, was written with an intention to love, to support, to be kind, to serve, to give and to help each and every one of you. My hope, is that you felt my energy, intentions and wishes that were infused through every word. Of course, like any process in life, while I was writing this, there were times when I felt fear, worry and frustration. My limiting beliefs showed up, so, I took a breath, became mindful, remembered that my thoughts and actions will create and manifest, I reconnected with my truth, my spirit, and it's intentions for this book. Once I found my connection, then and only then, did I take the next step forward. Some steps were small and some steps were more like giant leaps but as long as I was taking a step, I knew I would get this to you. One of my favourite quotes and one that I thought of often when writing this, is, *"Faith is taking the first step even when you don't see the whole staircase." - Martin Luther King Jr.*

I know that there are thousands of "self-help" books and courses out there, trust me, I have a rather large collection of them! I know that we are bombarded with "How-to's" and "How-not-to's", do it this way and to do it that way. With so much information out there, we can sometimes feel confused and overwhelmed. I do believe, that having access to more information is positive and serves us well, I also believe that we need to know how to feel into what is right for us, to know what our own internal guidance system is telling us, to know what way works for us, not because someone else told us, being able to go within and connect means you only need to take in what feels right for you. If it is right for you, at the core of your being, it is right for you.

There are too many books that make promises to change you. The book, can't change you. You are the only one. The book can guide you, can show you the wisdom or the information, you must choose it, you must choose to do the work. Meaningful change is a process. It can be uncomfortable when we are embracing our fears, uncertainty and change. Change happens by daily steps. Change happens by committing to being consistent. If we never learn how to bring the ideas and the information and make it work in our daily lives, all it is, is a really nice idea but we never get to see it in action, we never get to see the results of living a life from a place of love. We are missing out on so much if we don't take the ideas, take the knowledge and make it work today and every day. It takes courage to change. I know it is not easy but I also know that we all have the ability and the courage to create a life we dream of. It is there inside all of us, just bursting to come out. I hope that this book has inspired you in some small way to take action and has shown you how to bring more love, kindness, courage and compassion into your daily life. We are all living, breathing miracles and my hope is that you can see the miracle that you are and start to see each, and every day of your life as a miracle. Remember, a miracle is just a shift from fear to love. We all have the ability and the strength to make that shift, sometimes we just need a little push!

I conclude this piece of work, for now, with the utmost gratitude for all that were a part of this, seen and unseen. Firstly, I thank each and every one of you that is reading this now, thank you for your courage, thank you for your bravery and strength, thank you for being honest, open and willing and thank you for the gift that you are and the gifts that you have to share with the world. You are all so important to me, even though I may never meet you, I will forever be grateful for you. I hope I do get to meet some of you on the SOUL SIDE UP courses and workshops. Please come and connect, I would love to say thank you in person.

Thank you to all my teachers, healers, guides, seen, and unseen. I am forever a student and forever learning. Thank you for your teachings, thank you for showing me that the gift of teaching allows love to spread far and wide. Thank you to my angels, my Divine guides and St Therese (I will explain my relationship and love for this incredible Saint at a different time), You are my comfort, my support and my connection.

Thank you to all my clients that I work with on a daily basis, you inspire me, you allow me do what I was born to do by your openness and willingness and you teach me, thank you.

Thank you to all my family, friends and loved ones. You are my comfort, my support and my connection. You are the ones that listen and are present. Thank you for all your teachings. To my darling husband and children, you are unconditional love. Every day I thank God for you and all you do, all you are and all you ever will be. GRATEFUL.

Printed in Great Britain
by Amazon